A Journey to a Testimony

From Trials to Triumphs: A Walk with God

By

Carame Cameau

Preface

This book was inspired by my personal experiences and revelations in my walk with God. It chronicles the trials and triumphs I have faced, the lessons learned, and the deepened faith that has resulted. Through these pages, I aim to share my journey of transformation, demonstrating how God's grace and mercy have guided me through the darkest valleys to the mountain tops of testimony. My hope is that this story will inspire and encourage you to trust in His divine plan for your life.

The scriptures are from the KJV and amplified Bible.

Special Thanks

I thank God Almighty for allowing me to write this to testify His goodness. I also thank my son, Timothy Souverain, and my cousin, Phelet Cameau, for their unwavering support. Additionally, I extend my gratitude to my family, friends, and covenant brethren who have supported me in any form.

Introduction

How many times in our lives do we question the path we are on? Or think we are lost? Not knowing where we are headed can be frustrating and discouraging. Life often takes us down unknown roads that we did not see coming. Consequently, anxiety and fear set in, becoming snares in our journey.

Think about it: God knows us even beyond the womb of our mother. Our lives are predestined. Why should we think that life's surprises are surprises to Him as well? Each of us is on a different path. Our experiences in life differ, and our intimacy with God varies. For many, life is a journey toward a testimony.

When we find ourselves on these unknown roads, it's natural to feel apprehensive. The uncertainty can be overwhelming, and we may struggle to understand why certain things happen the way they do. We might question if we are on the right path or if we have strayed too far. However, it is important to remember that God's understanding and vision extend far beyond our limited perspective. He sees the entire picture, while we only catch glimpses.

This journey, with all its twists and turns, is not without purpose. Each experience, each challenge, and each triumph shapes us in ways we might not immediately recognize. These experiences are threads in the tapestry of our lives, intricately woven to form a unique and meaningful design.

Our intimacy with God varies because our journeys are unique. Some might feel a constant, close connection, while others might experience periods of distance and doubt. Yet, through it all, God's presence remains steadfast. He is always there, guiding us, even when we cannot see the way forward.

Embracing this perspective transforms our journey. Instead of viewing our challenges as obstacles, we can see them as opportunities for growth and deeper faith. Instead of succumbing to fear and anxiety, we can find peace in the knowledge that God is in control, that He has a plan, and that our lives are unfolding according to His divine purpose.

As we embark on this journey together, let us be prepared to learn, discover, and experience the profound ways in which God works in our lives. Let us be open to the lessons that each moment holds and trust that, no matter how uncertain the road ahead may seem, it leads us toward a greater testimony.

Join me in exploring this journey. Be prepared to delve into the experiences that shape me, the challenges that test me, and the faith that sustains me. Together, we will uncover the beauty of a life guided by God's hand through those pages.

A life that is ultimately a journey to a testimony.

About The Author

Carame Cameau was born in Haiti into a Christian and cultivated family. She is the youngest of 13 siblings. Carame completed her primary and secondary education in Haiti before migrating to the United States of America, where she earned a Bachelor of Science in Nursing from Chamberlain College of Nursing. She has worked in healthcare as a registered nurse for over a dozen years. She also earned her Master of Nursing Science degree at Nova Southeastern University in Florida, USA, and is certified as a family nurse practitioner and in functional medicine.

From a very young age, Carame was active in church activities, whether in the choir, individual groups, church cleaning, fasting, or midnight prayer. She was always at the forefront. The author is a devoted follower of Christ, whose life has been a testament to the power of faith, prayer, and God's unending grace.

Table of Contents

Chapter I: The ability to rely on God though there is unknown.

Trusting in God despite the unknown requires a profound faith and unwavering belief in His providence. In the face of uncertainty, the ability to rely on God is a testament to our faith and trust in His divine plan. Even when we cannot see the road ahead or comprehend the challenges we face, we anchor ourselves in the unwavering belief that God is with us, guiding our steps.

Trusting in God amidst the unknown is an act of surrender, acknowledging that His wisdom far surpasses our own and His ways are higher than our ways. It's a declaration of faith, affirming our confidence that He holds the future in His hands and will never leave nor forsake us.

In times of doubt and confusion, relying on God becomes our source of strength and assurance. We find comfort in His promises, knowing that He works all things together for our good, even when we cannot see the bigger picture.

Trusting in God despite the unknown is an invitation to walk by faith, not by sight. It's a journey of surrendering our fears and anxieties, and placing our hope and confidence in His unfailing love and faithfulness.

Ultimately, the ability to rely on God in the midst of uncertainty is a testament to the depth of our faith and the steadfastness of His presence in our lives. It's a journey of trust, courage, and unwavering belief in His promises, knowing that He is always with us, guiding us every step of the way.

It's understandable that we felt confused and frustrated by the lack of clarity about your condition and the appropriate course of action. When faced with health challenges, it's crucial to advocate for yourself and seek out the care that you need, even if it means pushing for further investigation or consulting with different specialists.

Depression and feelings of being overwhelmed can often accompany severe health issues, and it's essential to address both the physical and emotional aspects of your well-being. Seeking support from loved ones, as well as mental health professionals can be beneficial in navigating these difficult times.

Dreams can also be a way for our minds to process emotions and experiences, especially those related to loss and grief. It's natural to dream about loved ones who have passed away, and while it can be painful, it can also be a way to remind us that we are being consumed by our grief.

Remember to take care of yourself holistically – physically, mentally, and spiritually. Finding moments of peace and rest, practicing self-care, and seeking support when needed are all important steps in your journey toward healing and wellness. If you ever feel overwhelmed or unsure about your health, don't hesitate to reach out for help and guidance.

Indeed, finding solace in faith during challenging times can provide comfort and strength beyond measure. Trusting in a higher power to guide us through adversity can offer a sense of peace and assurance, even when circumstances seem overwhelming.

The journey of faith often involves facing uncertainties and navigating through difficult situations.

Yet, the belief in a divine presence that works for our good can sustain us through the darkest of times. As you mentioned, God has a way of turning our trials into testimonies, showcasing his faithfulness and grace.

Scriptures such as "come to me, all you who are weary and burdened, and I will give you rest" Matthew 11. remind us of the promise of divine support and comfort for those who seek it. In moments of distress, it's essential to lean on our faith, trusting that God hears our prayers and works on our behalf, even when we cannot see the immediate results.

Let's travel through those pages with me to experience how faith continues to be a source of strength and hope as I journey through life's challenges, and may you find healing and comfort in the presence of the Divine.

My parents in the U.S

After seven long years apart, the day finally arrived when my mother, Mrs Lodoine Cameau stepped foot into the USA. The joy of our reunion, especially with my mother, remains unmatched to this day. Besides God, I believe no one could love me more fiercely than she did. Her selflessness, particularly when it came to her children, was unparalleled, and I felt it most profoundly as the youngest child during our time together.

For the year that followed, I enjoyed my mother's presence in the USA immensely. I thanked God daily for allowing her to visit me. It was a pleasure to spoil her as much as I could. In my mind, I tirelessly imagined ways to take care of my parents, dreaming of a future where they would be comfortable and happy in their late years.

Months later, my father Mr, Lodoine Cameau also received his visa. Both my parents were now present with my sister and me in America. The joy was intense, and we celebrated every minute with them. Being able to eat my mother's cooking again was particularly enjoyable. Known by everyone who knew her for her cordon bleu cuisine, she prepared some of her delicious recipes for us. It was delightful to savor every piece of her meals.

They were also overjoyed to see my son, who was the child of their youngest. It was a blessing and grace from God to witness the joy of seeing my son with his maternal grandparents. The moments we shared were beyond satisfying. Watching my son enjoy his grandparents' company was deeply fulfilling and created memories I wanted to last forever.

These moments, filled with love and togetherness, were a testament to the bond we shared and the strength of our family. The time spent with my parents during this period was a precious gift, one that I cherished deeply and held close to my heart.

Celebration turns into nightmares

One memorable day, amidst our celebrations at my home, we decided to venture downtown to explore the city. Little did we know that our plans would take a tragic turn. In the car with us were my parents, an aunt, my ex-husband, and my two-year-old son. Just five minutes from home, we were involved in a harrowing car accident that would forever alter the trajectory of our lives. My father suffered severe injuries; his ribs and pelvis fractured, and he was rushed to the trauma ICU; his condition was critical. Throughout that agonizing night spent trembling in the hospital, consumed by fervent prayers for my father's survival, my mother remained a beacon of strength; her concern focused solely on my well-being amidst the chaos.

However, amidst the turmoil, accusations of negligence and personal gain surfaced among my siblings, plunging me into a whirlwind of emotional turmoil. All I ever wished for was to care for my parents in their twilight years, to repay their boundless love with the devotion they deserved. However, things took an unfortunate turn. From the hospital, they admitted my father to hospice after considering his case was terminal. Despite my fervent pleas and battles with the hospice team, my worst fears were realized as my father's health deteriorated rapidly, and my mother's condition took a grave turn.

In the depths of my despair, I pleaded, prayed, and fought tirelessly, beseeching God to spare my father's life. Amidst accusations of denial and grieving from others, I clung to hope with every fiber of my being. After several meetings with the hospice team. They agreed to transfer my papa back to another hospital under regular medical care. There, my dad's condition was treated. Eventually, my prayers were answered, and my father's condition improved enough for him to be discharged home, a walking, talking testament to the power of faith and perseverance.

The impact of the car accident

Yet, the impact of the accident, both physically and emotionally, continued to reverberate long after. My parents' journey to recovery was fraught with challenges, and the stress of it all weighed heavily on me. Nevertheless, little did I know, the most devastating chapter was yet to come.

In a cruel twist of fate, my worst fears materialized mere months later. Like Job's lament, "for the thing which I greatly feared has overtaken me," Job 3:25, tragedy struck with relentless force. Despite their initial recovery, my parents' return to Haiti proved to be the beginning of an unfathomable ordeal. Shortly after their arrival, my father suffered a debilitating fall, fracturing his hip in the process. Meanwhile, my mother's health took a drastic turn for the worse.

Desperate for life-saving treatment, I hastily arranged for my mother's transfer back to the USA. Upon arrival, she was immediately admitted to the hospital. However, her condition rapidly deteriorated, and she succumbed to heart and kidney failure within a mere two weeks of hospitalization.

During her hospitalization

During those two weeks, I visited her daily. Despite her severe diagnosis, she never gave the impression of someone who was dying. Each visit was filled with moments of joy and connection. We joked, shared stories, and reminisced about the past. Her laughter, loud and infectious, filled the room. I laugh the same way she did, and it was comforting to share that familiar sound with her during such a difficult time.

Even in her illness, we enjoyed each other's company as much as we could. Her strength and spirit shone through, providing both of us with precious moments of happiness amidst the uncertainty. Those days in the hospital, filled with laughter and love, are memories I hold dear, a testament to her incredible resilience and our unbreakable bond.

My last night with my mother

The memory of our last night together in the hospital is etched into my soul, a bittersweet tableau of laughter, storytelling, and shared moments of love. Yet, beneath the surface, an unspoken dread gnawed at me, foretelling the impending tragedy. I sat by her bed, singing and praying to God. In the middle of my worship, I was not at peace in my heart, which worried me that she might not survive this ordeal.

I longed to stay by her side throughout the night, but the needs of my young son tethered me to reality. As we bid her farewell in the dimly lit hospital corridor, little did I know that it would be our final goodbye. Promising to call her in the morning before rushing home, I never could have imagined the heart-wrenching news that awaited me at dawn.

The morning of the bad news

The morning of the bad news began with a flurry of missed calls, each one a harbinger of unspeakable loss. Dawn broke, and with it, a moment of terror descended upon me, plunging me into the depths of despair. I picked up my phone, seeing the long list of missed calls from the hospital. My heart sank; I feared something terrible had happened.

As I stared at the screen, the phone rang again. It was the hospital. Despite my fear, I knew I had to answer.

"Hello?" I said, my voice trembling.

A nurse rushed on the phone, her voice urgent and filled with sorrow. "Your mother died last night, just a few hours after you left the hospital. We tried to reach you but were unsuccessful."

To be honest, the rest of her words faded into a blur. The only phrase that echoed in my mind was "died last night."

After that call, everything went black. When my senses returned, I found myself on the floor. I was told I had passed out. I couldn't speak; the shock had taken my voice. It felt as if someone had dropped me into a land of darkness and torment.

Despite the overwhelming grief, I knew I had to stay strong for my father and siblings and fulfill my duties for the burial. We made the difficult decision to ship her body back to her natal land. The experience was beyond horrible, but in the midst of this profound loss, I found the strength to act.

The days that followed were a blur of arrangements and sorrow. My heart ached with the weight of the loss, but through it all, I held onto the belief that God was with me, guiding me through this darkest of times.

Return to her natal for funeral

Returning to Haiti with my mother's body for her funeral was a somber journey. The sight of my father confined to a wheelchair, his broken hip a physical manifestation of his broken heart, added to the weight of our collective grief. In his anguish, he pleaded with God to take him too, unable to fathom a life without his beloved wife by his side. His desperate pleas weighed heavily on me, as did his fervent wish for my mother's life to be spared.

Despite the heaviness of grief, I found strength in the midst of sorrow as I navigated the responsibilities of the funeral. I was determined to be a pillar of support for my father, who was devastated by the loss. The funeral was a poignant mix of sorrow and remembrance, honoring my mother's life and her immeasurable impact on those around her.

After the funeral

After the funeral, however, I was engulfed in a profound darkness that seemed insurmountable. The grief was relentless, and questions of life's purpose echoed in my mind, grappling with the incomprehensible reality of death's inevitability. The loss of my mother, compounded by my father's intense grief and physical ailment, left me questioning everything.

Navigating this period was incredibly challenging. I tried to immerse myself in daily routines— greeting people who visited, and engaged in household duties—but the sorrow was ever-present, an unshakeable shadow. It felt as if I was carrying an invisible weight, a constant reminder of the loved one I had lost and the fragility of life itself.

In these moments of deep despair, I leaned heavily on my faith and the memories of my mother's strength and resilience. Her unwavering love and the lessons she imparted became my guiding light. Though the darkness was profound, the love for my son, along with my faith, helped me slowly begin to find my way through the grief.

This journey through loss and sorrow, while deeply painful, also reaffirmed the importance of cherishing every moment with loved ones and holding onto the strength that comes from faith and community. It reminded me that even in the face of profound darkness, there is a way forward, illuminated by the love and memories of those who have passed and the support of those who remain.

Back to the USA

Upon returning to the USA from my mother's funeral, I tried to immerse myself back into my daily life—college, work, exercise, and household duties. On the surface, I acted as if everything was okay, but inside, my heart was aching. I was in despair, and it felt like no one could understand the depths of my sorrow.

However, I convinced myself that I must go on. My mother would not want me to renounce my dreams and my family just because she was no longer around to support me. Though it was easier said than done, I continued to put one foot in front of the other and fulfill my role in my household. I took on a heavy load, enrolling in five classes in one semester and working seven days a week. I intentionally filled every moment of my time, believing that keeping busy would reduce the pain and sorrow I was enduring.

Despite this frantic pace, the grief was ever-present, lingering beneath the surface of my daily routines. Each task, each assignment, and each work shift was a temporary distraction from the overwhelming loss I felt. I didn't want to leave any space for me to think, fearing that without constant activity, the full weight of my sorrow would become unbearable.

Through it all, I held onto the belief that my mother would want me to persevere. The memory of her strength and resilience became my guiding force, encouraging me to keep moving forward despite the profound emptiness I felt inside. The process was incredibly challenging, but each step I took was a testament to her enduring influence on my life.

Attention

Know that everyone is different and that people grieve in unique ways. What might seem light and easy to navigate for one person could be incredibly challenging for someone else. In my case, I spent seven years apart from my parents. As the youngest child, I had the least amount of time with them. God, I loved them dearly, and I cherished every moment in their presence. My mother's passing was particularly hard for me to navigate.

Another tragedy struck

One afternoon, while I was in class, my phone rang. It was a call from Haiti. It was only two months after my mother's burial. Knowing my father was ill, I felt a surge of anxiety. I ran out of the classroom to answer the call. It was my eldest sister on the line, and she told me that our father would not make it. Desperately, I told her to put him on the phone.

"Pay," I called him by his nickname.

"Zou," he responded with my nickname.

Those were his last words before he expired right there on the phone.

Standing on the balcony of the classroom, I felt numb. I wanted to cry, but my entire being was paralyzed. The overwhelming toll of my mother's death was already heavy on me, and now, losing my father felt unbearable. I wondered if I could endure all this pain and continue living.

Another tragedy struck when my father passed away. The passing of my mother had left him with an empty soul, pleading with God to take him as well to be with his beloved wife. He had often expressed his desire to die before my mother, which only added to my trauma when I lost the battle to save her. Despite my quick actions to get her to the hospital, my efforts were unsuccessful.

The burden of grief weighed heavily on my heart, but through it all, I remembered the strength and resilience my parents had instilled in me. In the midst of sorrow, I held onto my faith, believing that God would guide me through this storm. Their memories became my source of strength, propelling me forward despite the overwhelming despair.

For three agonizing years, grief consumed me, manifesting in nightly dreams of my mother and tear-stained moments of solitude. Despite the facade of composure, I presented to the world, I was fractured inside, lost in a labyrinth of pain and confusion. Yet, amidst the darkness, I clung to the strength that God had bestowed upon me, masking my inner turmoil with a veneer of happiness and composure.

However, the toll of this internal battle was undeniable, threatening to unravel me emotionally, physically, and spiritually in the long run. The facade of strength I wore was a fragile shield against the relentless onslaught of grief, a facade that would inevitably crumble under the weight of my sorrow.

How can we avoid the mistake of turning away from God when faced with life's tragedies?

When facing the tragedies of life, it's common for individuals to experience feelings of anger, confusion, and despair, which may lead them to question their faith or distance themselves from God. However, there are several ways to avoid making the mistake of running away from God during times of hardship: for God says: "Come to me all who are weary and burdened, and I will give you rest" Matthew 11:28

Allow yourself to feel and process your emotions without judgment by acknowledging your emotions. It's normal to experience a range of feelings, including anger, sadness, and doubt, during difficult times.

It is good to seek support. Surround yourself with supportive friends, family members, or members of your religious community who can provide comfort, guidance, and understanding. Sharing your burdens with others can help alleviate feelings of isolation and strengthen your faith.

It is imperative to engage in prayer and reflection. Use prayer as a means of communication with God, expressing your thoughts, concerns, and struggles openly and honestly, though it will not be easy. Furthermore, engage in regular reflection and meditation to find solace and spiritual guidance in the midst of adversity.

While it may be challenging, try to find meaning and purpose in your suffering. Reflect on how your experiences can deepen your faith, strengthen your character, and foster empathy and compassion for others.

Cultivate a mindset of gratitude by acknowledging the blessings and moments of grace in your life, even amidst hardship. Recognizing God's presence in the midst of adversity can help nurture a sense of spiritual resilience.

Turn to sacred texts, inspirational literature, or spiritual teachings for guidance and encouragement. Allow the wisdom and insights found in these resources to provide comfort and perspective during difficult times. Refuse to forsake your attending church. Stay actively engaged with your faith community by attending church services, participating in spiritual fellowships, or seeking guidance from religious leaders. Surrounding yourself with a supportive community can provide strength and encouragement on your spiritual journey.

One of the most important things is to release feelings of resentment, bitterness, or anger toward God or others by practicing forgiveness. Forgiveness is a powerful spiritual practice that can help heal wounds and cultivate inner peace.

By practicing these strategies and remaining open to the presence of God in your life, you can navigate the trials of life with faith, resilience, and spiritual growth.

Chapter II: Life without my parents

Now that my parents have passed away, life feels utterly devoid of meaning. As if to compound my grief, my marriage was unraveling before my eyes. Despite these overwhelming challenges, I found an unexpected wellspring of strength from God. I was determined to complete my first college degree, all while shouldering the responsibility of raising my 2-year-old son.

Amidst the tumult of my personal life, I remained steadfast in my pursuit of academic excellence. Graduating with distinction became a beacon of hope in the midst of my pain. Education became my sanctuary, providing a sense of purpose and a much-needed distraction from the turmoil surrounding me. Balancing the demands of work and school became my refuge, shielding me from the full weight of my grief.

The departure of my parents inflicted an indescribable level of stress upon me. Yet, what struck me the most was the apparent inability of those around me to perceive the profound anguish I was grappling with internally. Even within the comforting embrace of church, surrounded by family and friends, my silent suffering went unnoticed, leaving me feeling isolated and unseen.

Soon after, I made the decision to enroll in nursing school. Despite my determination to move forward, my deceased mother continued to occupy my thoughts, visiting me nightly in my dreams. Strangely, I found solace in these dreams, as they provided me with a sense of closeness to her that I desperately craved. It was as if releasing her from my spirit would be a betrayal of our bond, so I held onto her memory tightly, refusing to let go.

While I threw myself into the demands of school, work, and caring for my son, internally, I was crumbling. The weight of grief, coupled with the relentless pace of life, created a toxic blend of emotions that threatened to consume me. I was keenly aware that this combination of unresolved feelings and conditions could lead to physical illness if left unaddressed. Yet, despite this awareness, I struggled to find a way to heal the wounds festering within me.

To maintain my sanity amidst the chaos of my life, I established a daily routine that included regular exercise and dedicated study sessions for school. These activities served as anchors, grounding me in the present moment and providing a sense of purpose and structure. Despite the darkness that seemed to loom over my future, I clung to a glimmer of hope, struggling to envision a brighter tomorrow.

Throughout it all, one thing remained constant—I never abandoned church. Even in moments of doubt and despair, I found solace within the walls of the church. It became my sanctuary, a safe haven where I could seek refuge from the storms raging within me. There, amidst the flickering candles and hushed prayers, I felt a sense of peace wash over me, if only for a fleeting moment. Despite my wavering faith and unanswered questions, I continued to turn to God, trusting that He would guide me through the darkness.

The death of my siblings

Losing my first sibling.

Following my parents' deaths, the cycle of loss continued relentlessly. One of my brothers "Omenais Cameau" was found dead in his bed, the cause still unknown. I didn't have the chance to pay my last respects to him, which was devastating. He was the closest to me. We grew up mostly in the capital together, unlike our other siblings, who partially grew up in the village. He was one of the most cultivated men in our family, a person of great intellect and refinement.

Losing him has left a profound void in my life. His presence was a constant source of comfort and companionship. The pain of his sudden and unexplained departure is a heavy burden, but I find solace in the memories we shared and in the hope that he is at peace. My faith sustains me through this dark time, reminding me that God's mercy and grace will eventually bring healing.

Second sibling passing

Soon after, within a year of my brother's death, another brother "Caleb Cameau" passed away. This brother was one of the oldest and was a preacher who dedicated his life to teaching people about the things of God. Faithful in his service to the Lord, he participated in the church choir, led early morning services, and fearlessly preached alone in the streets at dawn. A true servant of God, I know he is now resting in the divine.

I was told he was the one who used to babysit me the most as a baby. My time spent with him was always about the Bible and his personal experiences with God. He used to be the tenor in the choir. Among all the singers, his voice could be easily distinguished. He was a gifted servant of God. Whether it was preaching, singing, or leading prayer groups, his dedication was incredible.

The loss of these two brothers, both so integral to my life and my faith, has been an immense sorrow. Yet, I find strength in my faith, knowing they are with God and that their lives were a testament to His glory.

Third sibling passing

A few years later, tragedy struck again when a third brother, Yonel Cameau" was involved in a terrible motorcycle accident and died untimely. He was the bravest man in our family, a fearless person undaunted by anything. He was strong, tall, and handsome. Yet he died mysteriously in a so-called motorcycle accident near the gate of his village. Meanwhile, I began experiencing severe symptoms myself.

Fourth sibling passing

About a year after my third brother's death, tragedy hit once more. My eldest sister "Midoude Cameau" who had been planning another visit to the USA after many previous visits, did not make it this time. I spoke to her on the phone one night, and the rest is history. She had a stroke the next day. She died 24 hours later at the nearest hospital. At that time, I was in the middle of facing my own storms, horribly sick, with the medical team struggling to pinpoint a diagnosis. Plus, I was in the middle of completing my master's program. How much can a heart bear? Only God knows.

The loss of my siblings, each unique in their virtues and roles, added layers of grief and hardship. It was a time of immense suffering and sorrow, testing the very limits of my endurance. Yet, through each tragic event, I was reminded of the fragility of life and the strength that comes from faith. These experiences, painful as they were, became part of the journey leading to my testimony of God's sustaining grace and the hope that lies beyond our earthly trials.

What you need to know

In the depths of my despair, I turned to the pages of my journals, pouring out my heart to God in tear-stained prayers. "Why me?" I cried, grappling with the weight of my trials and tribulations. All I had ever wanted was to serve Him faithfully, yet it seemed that the cascade of challenges crashing down upon me showed no mercy. The death of my parents, three older brothers, one sister, and a failed marriage crippled me. Little did I know that the call of God upon someone's life could stir up turmoil, inciting confusion and opposition from the forces of darkness. They are things of God; one will never understand.

Clarification: The call of God does not cause death and turmoil in someone's life. Rather, we are predestined to be in those situations as training sessions for the specific path that God has chosen for His elected servants. David says, "For You formed my inward parts and You knitted me together in my mother's womb." —Psalms 139.

As I wrestled with my faith and questioned the purpose behind my suffering, I came to understand a profound truth: the greater the calling, the fiercer the attacks. It became clear that my struggles were not merely random misfortunes but rather the inevitable consequences of answering God's call to a higher purpose. From an early age, I knew I was chosen for the service of God. At just 13 or 14 years old, I could lead an entire night watch service for three nights in a row without slumbering, fully devoted to His work, so to mention that.

Reflecting on my childhood, I recalled a recurring dream that had haunted me for years. In it, I found myself pursued by a herd of massive cows with menacing horns, their thunderous hooves pounding relentlessly behind me. In my terror, I would flee, seeking refuge in the safety of the trees, yet never daring to confront the source of my fear head-on.

It dawned on me that, much like in my dream, I had spent much of my life running from my destiny rather than embracing it. Despite harboring lofty aspirations and grand ambitions, I often found myself paralyzed by fear when it came time to take action. The gap between my dreams and reality seemed insurmountable, leaving me feeling overwhelmed and defeated.

Yet, in the midst of my turmoil, a glimmer of hope emerged. I began to realize that my struggles were not a sign of weakness, but rather a testament to the magnitude of the calling placed upon my life. With this newfound understanding, I resolved to face my fears head-on, trusting in God's guidance to lead me on the path to fulfilling my destiny.

Chapter III: Initial symptoms

I made a dedicated effort to regain control of my health. I committed to walking 3-4 hours, four times a week, combined with adopting a healthier diet. As a result, I successfully shed over 20 pounds, feeling optimistic about my progress.

However, one day, during my routine walk, everything changed. Within just 10 minutes, I was overwhelmed by severe epigastric pain and palpitations in my neck, leaving me bewildered and in distress. Despite my best efforts to understand what was happening, the situation remained perplexing, and my condition did not improve.

Seeking answers, I decided to visit the hospital. Tests revealed elevated cardiac enzymes, prompting a consultation with a cardiologist. Surprisingly, the cardiologist concluded that my symptoms were gastrointestinal in nature, rather than cardiac. I found myself engulfed in confusion, unable to advocate for myself as I would for my own patients. Questions swirled in my mind—was my digestive the root cause? Why had not a Gastrointestinal doctor been consulted initially?

Discharged with minimal investigation into my elevated cardiac enzymes or abdominal issues, I returned home feeling somewhat relieved. Adjusting my diet brought some relief, but lingering symptoms persisted, including heartburn, epigastric pain, and a swollen abdomen, draining my energy and leaving me in a state of despair.

Consulting a new primary doctor provided little solace, as the focus remained on routine blood tests, x-rays, and young age rather than my pressing concerns. Despite their reassurances to maintain a healthy lifestyle, I found myself blindly trusting their advice, echoing the cautionary proverb, "Malheur à l'homme qui se confie en l'homme" (Woe to the man who trusts in man).

Months passed before I could secure an appointment with a gastrointestinal specialist. Meanwhile, I endured worsening symptoms, trapped in a cycle of physical discomfort and mental anguish. The subsequent endoscopic examination yielded no significant findings, leaving me grappling with uncertainty and despair.

Reflecting on this challenging journey, I realized I was trapped in a state of depression and helplessness, unable to draw upon my professional knowledge or find respite from the darkness enveloping me. Each day felt like an uphill battle, draining me mentally, physically, and spiritually.

Even in my sleep, I found no solace, haunted by dreams of lost loved ones, particularly my mother, whose passing left an indelible mark on my soul. Wrestling with grief, I struggled to find solace in the scriptural admonition against worldly sorrow without hope, striving to honor God's will amidst the pain.

Though the journey has been arduous, I cling to the belief that every trial serves a purpose, ultimately glorifying the name of the Lord

Praise be to God, who remains steadfast by the side of His children, even in the midst of trials and tribulations. Though His presence may sometimes seem elusive, He tirelessly works on our behalf, turning our struggles into testimonies of His grace and faithfulness.

In the face of daunting challenges, it's easy for confusion and doubt to cloud our minds, leaving us vulnerable to the schemes of the enemy. The weight of our circumstances may even make it difficult to reach out to God, yet He promises to provide rest and solace to those who are weary and burdened.

Even when we feel helpless and powerless, God's intervention is never far away. He sees our struggles and hears our cries for help, ready to extend His comforting hand and guide us through the darkest of times.

As we navigate the perilous journey of life, let us cling to the assurance that God is ever-present, working all things together for our good. Let us find solace in His promise of rest for the weary, knowing that His love and mercy will sustain us through every trial and hardship.

The start of undeniable symptoms

A year later, As I ventured into the realm of nursing, my heart brimming with a desire to serve others and lay the foundation for my entrepreneurial dreams, I found myself swept up in the whirlwind of my burgeoning career. Amidst the chaos of hospital corridors and the clamor of patient needs, I scarcely had a moment to pause and tend to the whispers of my own body.

Yet, amidst the clamor of my professional pursuits, there were whispers, subtle reminders from within, that all was not well. Palpitations in my heart, like fleeting whispers in the cacophony of life, would occasionally seize my attention, only to be brushed aside in the relentless pursuit of my goals. Attributing these bodily signals to the inevitable stresses and strains of the profession, I soldiered on, determined to achieve my goals.

It was easy, perhaps too easy, to dismiss these signs as mere manifestations of fatigue or stress. After all, in a field as demanding and fast-paced as nursing, it was all too common to sacrifice one's own well-being in service to others. Yet, as the whispers grew louder and more insistent, I could no longer ignore the subtle cries of my own body, pleading for attention amidst the chaos of my professional endeavors.

In the midst of administering care to others, I realized the importance of heeding the call to self-care—listening to the whispers of my own body and soul. For how could I hope to offer compassion and healing to others if I neglected the well-being of my own being?

Thus began my journey of self-discovery and self-care, a journey marked by moments of introspection and vulnerability amidst the relentless demands of my career. And though the path ahead may be fraught with challenges and uncertainties, I am determined to honor the whispers of my own body, to nurture the flame of my own well-being amidst the hustle and bustle of my professional pursuits. For intending to the whispers within, I find the strength and resilience to continue my journey with compassion, grace, and authenticity.

It wasn't until a year later that the gravity of my symptoms could no longer be ignored. What had initially seemed like minor disturbances in my health had evolved into persistent concerns that demanded attention. I noticed a swollen abdomen and feet. I experienced shortness of breath within a few steps, let alone climbing the stairs. With a heavy heart and a tinge of trepidation, I scheduled a routine visit to the medical office, hoping for reassurance and relief.

Yet, as I sat in the sterile confines of the examination room, awaiting the medical doctor, a sense of unease settled over me like a heavy fog. Despite the outward facade of calm composure, inwardly, I wrestled with a rising tide of fear and uncertainty. What if something far more sinister lurked beneath the surface? What if the invisible adversary I faced proved to be insurmountable?

As the minutes stretched into eternity, each second weighed heavily upon my soul, amplifying the quiet whispers of doubt and dread that gnawed at the edges of my consciousness. And when the doctor finally entered the room, I braced myself for the worst, steeling my resolve against whatever fate awaited me.

To my dismay, the blood tests showed no apparent dysfunction, no glaring abnormalities to explain the symptoms that had plagued me for so long. And yet, despite the reassurance of the medical professionals, I could not shake the lingering sense of unease that gripped my heart like a vice.

In that moment of uncertainty, I turned to the one source of solace that had never failed me: prayer. With fervent urgency, I poured out my fears and anxieties before the throne of grace, seeking refuge in the embrace of the Divine. And though the invisible adversary I faced seemed formidable and daunting, I clung to the promise of God's steadfast presence, trusting that He would guide me through the darkest of valleys.

Little did I know that this moment of uncertainty would mark the beginning of a journey fraught with challenges and obstacles, yet imbued with a sense of divine purpose and providence. And though the road ahead may be fraught with uncertainty, I walk forward with unwavering faith, knowing that I am not alone, for the One who holds the stars in His hands walks beside me, lighting the way with His grace and love.

As my symptoms continued to escalate, casting a shadow of uncertainty over my well-being, I knew that I could no longer face this battle alone. Fearing the worst, I turned to my close family members and a trusted friend, confiding in them the gravity of my situation and the urgency of taking action.

Together, we deliberated on the best course of action, weighing the options before us with a sense of urgency and determination. With each passing moment, my symptoms intensified, casting a pall of fear and anxiety over our collective resolve. It was clear that decisive action was needed, and we concluded that a visit to the emergency room was not only prudent but necessary.

As my son and I made our way to the hospital where I worked as a registered nurse, a tumult of emotions churned within me, mingling with a steely resolve to confront whatever lay ahead. The journey to the emergency room was fraught with uncertainty, each step forward a testament to the strength of my resolve and the unwavering support of my loved ones by my side.

Arriving at the hospital, I braced myself for what lay ahead, steeling my nerves against the unknown. With each passing moment, my symptoms loomed larger in my mind, casting a shadow of doubt and fear over my fragile sense of hope. And yet, amidst the chaos and uncertainty, there remained a glimmer of hope, a flicker of resilience that refused to be extinguished. Once again, the medical team revealed that nothing appeared abnormal based on the blood tests and examination. 'Just go and continue to see your specialists,' they said.

In that moment of vulnerability, I found strength in the embrace of my loved ones and the unwavering support of my colleagues. And though the road ahead may be fraught with challenges and uncertainties, I walk forward with renewed hope and determination, knowing that I am not alone in this fight.

Replacing anxiety with fear and love for God.

Replacing anxiety with fear and love for God involves shifting your focus from worry and fear to trust and faith in a higher power, thereby cultivating within yourself a greater sense of peace and love for God. Start by reminding yourself that God has a plan for you and that everything happens for a reason, trusting in God's wisdom and guidance even when things seem uncertain or challenging.

Surrender your worries and fears to God through prayer and meditation, letting go of the need to control every outcome, and trusting that God will take care of you. Cultivate an attitude of gratitude by focusing on the blessings in your life, taking time each day to thank God for the good things, both big and small, and acknowledging His presence in your life. When anxious thoughts arise, consciously replace them with positive affirmations and scriptures that remind you of God's love and protection, repeating these affirmations regularly to reinforce positive thinking patterns.

Practice mindfulness by staying present in the moment, focusing on what you can do right now to align with God's will and live in His grace rather than worrying about the future or dwelling on the past. Avoid isolation, as it is the plan of the enemy to deprive you of well-being, and engage in spiritual practices such as prayer, meditation, reading scripture, and attending church services. Seek support from a spiritual community or mentor who can offer guidance, encouragement, and prayer support during times of anxiety or doubt.

Finally, focus on serving others and showing love and compassion to those in need, as acts of service can shift your focus away from your own worries and help you experience the joy of making a positive difference in the lives of others. These practices can help deepen your connection with God and cultivate a sense of peace and love.

Chapter IV: Emergency visit experience

As I arrived at the hospital. The initial encounter with the emergency room staff left me feeling disheartened and dismissed, as my pleas for help seemed to fall on deaf ears. Despite the urgency of my situation, I was met with skepticism and indifference, as the staff cited my status as under the care of a primary physician, dismissing the severity of my symptoms.

Frustrated and desperate for answers, I refused to be silenced, determined to be heard in the face of my escalating distress. Gathering my resolve, I made the bold decision to reveal my identity as a fellow healthcare professional, hoping that this revelation would lend credence to the urgency of my situation.

Finally acknowledged, I was ushered into the inner sanctum of the emergency room, where a team of medical professionals sprang into action, conducting a battery of tests and imaging procedures with a sense of urgency and purpose. With each passing moment, the gravity of my situation became increasingly apparent, as the results of the tests revealed a cascade of alarming abnormalities that painted a bleak picture of my health.

As the medical team worked tirelessly to unravel the mystery of my symptoms, I found myself grappling with a whirlwind of emotions, ranging from fear and anxiety to frustration and despair. And yet, amidst the chaos and uncertainty, there remained a glimmer of hope, a steadfast belief that answers would soon be forthcoming, and that a path to healing would be revealed.

In that moment of vulnerability, I clung to the unwavering support of my loved ones and the dedication of the medical professionals who were committed to guiding me through the storm. And though the road ahead may be fraught with challenges and uncertainties, I walk forward with renewed determination, knowing that I am not alone in this fight, and that together, we will confront whatever lies ahead with courage and resilience.

As the medical team delved deeper into the labyrinth of my symptoms, their efforts were met with frustration and uncertainty, as they struggled to pinpoint a definitive diagnosis. Despite their expertise and diligence, the elusive nature of my condition remained shrouded in mystery, leaving me and my loved ones grappling with a sense of unease and apprehension.

And yet, amidst the uncertainty that loomed over me like a dark cloud, I found myself enveloped in a sense of peace that defied logic and reason. It was as if a quiet assurance settled over me, whispering words of comfort and reassurance in the midst of the storm. In the depths of my soul, I clung to the unwavering belief that everything would ultimately be alright, that a path to healing would reveal itself in due time.

Developing the ability to focus

Developing the ability to focus on your spiritual life can deepen your connection with your beliefs, enhance your sense of purpose, and provide a source of strength and guidance in challenging times. Here are some strategies to help you cultivate focus in your spiritual journey:

Seek to clarify your spiritual goals and intentions. Reflect on what aspects of your spiritual life you want to deepen or explore further, whether it is prayer, worship, fellowship, and so on. Setting clear intentions can help you stay focused and motivated on your path.

Establish a dedicated sacred space in your home where you can engage in spiritual practices, such as closet, bathroom, living room, kitchen, or bedroom. For me, it is a bench in my bedroom on the side of my bed where I sit or kneel to pray. This space can serve as a sanctuary where you can disconnect from distractions and focus on nurturing your spiritual connection.

Aim to practice regular prayer and meditation. Incorporate meditation into your daily routine to quiet the mind, cultivate inner peace, and deepen your spiritual awareness. Choose a meditation technique that resonates with you, as Psalm 1 says: 'Meditate day and night.'

Set aside time for prayer or engage in warfare that is meaningful to you, such as 30 minutes' devotion early in the morning or prior to bedtime. Whether it's reciting traditional prayers, lighting candles, or performing ceremonial rituals, these practices can help center your focus and foster a sense of connection with the divine.

Dive in sacred texts of the bible. Dedicate time to study and reflect on sacred texts from your spiritual tradition. Study the teachings, stories, and wisdom contained within these texts, and contemplate how they apply to your own life journey.

Stay connected with your spiritual community. Surround yourself with like-minded individuals who share your spiritual beliefs and values. Like myself, I only talked with a few people of faith during those afflicted times. In fact, that kept me grounded in my faith. Engage in spiritual communities, whether it's attending local church services, participating in prayer groups, or joining online churches. Sharing your journey with others can provide support, inspiration, and accountability.

Thrive to cultivate an attitude of gratitude by regularly acknowledging and appreciating the blessings in your life. Psalms 103, be grateful to God in all circumstances. Gratitude practices can help shift your focus away from negativity and towards a more positive and uplifted mindset.

Do not hesitate to spend time in nature to reconnect with the beauty and wonder of the natural world. Whether it's taking a walk in the woods, sitting by a lake, or gardening, immersing yourself in nature can be a powerful way to quiet the mind and open your heart to the divine presence of God

Practice mindfulness in your daily activities by bringing your full attention to the present moment. Whether you're eating, walking, or interacting with others, strive to be fully present and attentive, allowing yourself to experience the richness of each moment.

Trust that your spiritual journey is unfolding exactly as it should be. Embrace the ups and downs, the doubts and uncertainties, knowing that each experience is an opportunity for growth and learning.

By incorporating these strategies into your spiritual practice and making them a consistent part of your life, you can cultivate a deeper sense of focus, meaning, and connection in your spiritual journey.

Chapter V: Hospital stay reflection

As the days stretched into a week, I remained hospitalized under the watchful eye of the medical team, undergoing a battery of tests and procedures in search of answers. Also, I was medicated for body fluid control. Though the road ahead remained fraught with uncertainty, I found comfort in the unwavering support of my loved ones, who stood by my side with unwavering devotion and compassion.

And then, after seven long days of uncertainty and apprehension, the moment of reckoning arrived. With a heavy heart and a sense of resignation, I was discharged from the hospital, tasked with seeking further evaluation from specialists in the hopes of unraveling the mystery of my condition.

As I stepped out into the world beyond the confines of the hospital walls, I carried with me a sense of peace that transcended the uncertainty of my circumstances. For in the depths of my soul, I knew that I was not alone, that the Holy Spirit was guiding me through the storm, and that everything would ultimately be alright. With this unwavering faith as my anchor, I embarked on the next leg of my journey, fortified by the love and support of those who walked beside me.

As my journey continued and the days turned into months, the mystery surrounding my illness only seemed to deepen. Despite the gradual improvement of my symptoms, the underlying cause remained elusive, evading the grasp of medical professionals and leaving those closest to me perplexed and concerned.

With each passing day, the uncertainty of my condition casts a shadow of doubt and apprehension over my life, clouding my thoughts and stirring whispers of fear and speculation. Despite the best efforts of medical professionals to unravel the mystery, the answers remained frustratingly out of reach, leaving us all grasping at straws in search of a solution.

Faced with the enigma of my illness, speculation ran rampant, fueled by fear and uncertainty. Some whispered of supernatural forces at play, invoking tales of unseen powers and malevolent spirits. Others sought solace in more rational explanations, clinging to the hope that science would eventually prevail and uncover the truth behind my symptoms.

Yet, amidst the uncertainty and speculation, one thing remained clear: the unwavering support and love of those who stood by my side. Through the darkest moments of my journey, they remained steadfast in their devotion, offering words of encouragement and prayers of hope as we navigated the uncertain waters together.

And though the road ahead may be fraught with challenges and uncertainties, I am buoyed by the knowledge that I do not walk this path alone. For in the midst of the mystery and the unknown, there is a glimmer of hope that shines bright, guiding us forward with courage and resilience. And with each step we take, we draw closer to the truth, trusting that answers will be revealed in due time, and that healing will come to light.

In the midst of the chaos and confusion that engulfed my life, I found myself standing at a crossroads, grappling with the unknown while holding fast to my unwavering belief in Jesus Christ. Despite the uncertainty that loomed over me like a dark cloud, I remained steadfast in my conviction that God would see me through, guiding me towards healing and wholeness even in the midst of the storm.

As I contemplated the suggestion to relocate to another state, I found myself torn between the familiarity of home and the allure of new beginnings. The prospect of leaving behind everything I knew and venturing into the unknown filled me with a sense of trepidation, yet amidst the uncertainty, I found solace in the unshakeable foundation of my faith.

For no matter where life's journey may lead, I knew that my faith would serve as an unwavering beacon of hope in the darkest of times. It was the rock upon which I stood, the anchor that held me steady amidst the tempest of life's storms. And though the road ahead may be fraught with challenges and uncertainties, I took comfort in the knowledge that I was not alone, for the One who walked beside me would never leave nor forsake me.

With each step forward, I leaned into my faith, trusting that God would guide my footsteps and lead me toward a brighter tomorrow. As I embarked on this new chapter of my journey, I did so with courage and conviction, knowing that no matter what trials may lie ahead, my faith would be my strength, my refuge, and my constant companion.

Reflecting on a midnight prayer session

The scripture from Proverbs 22:6, "train up a child in the way he should go, and when he is old he will not depart from it," resonated deeply within me, serving as a testament to the foundation of faith upon which I had been raised. From a young age, I had been immersed in the ways of God, surrounded by the fervent prayers of my parents, who turned to Him in times of tribulation and trial.

Their unwavering faith left an indelible mark on my soul, shaping my understanding of who God is and how He works in the lives of His children. As I witnessed their steadfast reliance on prayer in the face of adversity, I learned that true strength lies not in our own abilities but in our dependence on the Almighty.

Through the example set by my parents, I came to understand that prayer is not just a ritual or obligation but a powerful tool for spiritual warfare. It is through prayer that we align ourselves with the will of God and invite His presence to dwell within us, guiding us through life's challenges and triumphs.

As I continue to walk this journey of faith, I am grateful for the foundation of prayer that has been laid before me. And though the path may be fraught with obstacles and uncertainties, I take comfort in the knowledge that I am never alone, for His spirit dwells within me, guiding me every step of the way.

In the midst of my spiritual warfare, I made a conscious decision to confront the enemy head-on, armed with the unwavering belief that God would never abandon me. With these words of faith as my shield, I embarked on a journey of prayer and spiritual warfare, trusting in the promise that God's presence would never wane.

I recall one pivotal moment in this journey occurred during a midnight prayer session at Pastor Wendell's church. As I poured out my heart before the Lord, seeking His guidance and protection, I was overcome by a profound encounter with the divine. In the stillness of that sacred space, a voice spoke to me with clarity and conviction, declaring, "Carame, do not fear, for I will never leave you nor forsake you."

Tears welled up in my eyes as the weight of those words washed over me. Though I was young and inexperienced in matters of prophetic ministry at that time, I could not deny the undeniable truth of His presence. In that moment, surrounded by the comforting embrace of God's love, I felt a sense of peace and reassurance, unlike anything I had ever known.

As a Baptist Christian, I had been raised in the traditions of my faith, but this encounter transcended the confines of religious doctrine, speaking directly to the depths of my soul. Though I may not have fully understood the significance of what had transpired, I knew without a doubt that God was with me, guiding me every step of the way.

In the years that followed, I continued to walk in faith, drawing strength from the assurance that God's promises are true and His presence is ever-present. Though the road ahead may be fraught with challenges and uncertainties, I take comfort in the knowledge that I am never alone, for He walks beside me, leading me onward in His perfect love.

The secret of connecting with powerful servants of God

Amidst the struggle to find my voice in prayer, I stumbled upon a beacon of light in the form of Bishop Duncan-Williams, a man of God whose teachings on YouTube ignited a flame of hope within me. Night after night, I immersed myself in his sessions of warfare prayers, allowing his words to penetrate the depths of my soul and stir a fervent desire to communicate with the divine.

These nightly sessions became a lifeline for me, a source of inspiration and strength in the midst of my spiritual battles. Through Bishop Duncan's teachings, I not only learned the importance of prayer at night but also discovered how to engage in spiritual warfare, fighting against the unseen forces that sought to hinder my faith.

As I immersed myself in Bishop Duncan's nightly prayers, declaring and decreeing the promises of God, I felt a profound renewal of strength within me. Despite the decline in my physical health, my faith soared to new heights with each prayer uttered in the quiet of the night. Night after night, I found solace and inspiration in his teachings, drawing closer to God in fervent prayer.

It was during this time of spiritual awakening that I felt a prompting from the Holy Spirit to delve deeper into the scriptures, particularly the accounts of the prophets in the Old Testament. With a sense of divine guidance, I began to explore the prophetic writings of Joel and others, seeking to uncover the timeless truths hidden within their words.

However, it was the book of Isaiah that captivated my heart and soul like no other. Every time I turned its sacred pages, tears streamed down my face, as if the very presence of God permeated the words written on the ancient parchment. In the prophetic verses of Isaiah, I found echoes of God's unfailing love and boundless grace, a love so profound that it moved me to my core.

As I journeyed through the pages of Isaiah, I was reminded time and again of God's faithfulness to His people, even in the midst of their darkest trials and tribulations. His promises rang out like a clarion call, reassuring me of His steadfast presence and unwavering love.

In the midst of my own struggles and uncertainties, I found comfort and assurance in the timeless truths revealed through the prophet Isaiah. Through his words, I was reminded that God's love knows no bounds, reaching down to lift me up in my times of need. And as tears of gratitude and awe flowed freely from my eyes, I was filled with a deep conviction that indeed, God loves me, and His love will sustain me through every trial and triumph that lies ahead.

Chapter VI: Connecting with the prophets

Prophet TB Joshua

As I persisted in my nightly warfare prayers with Bishop Duncan-Williams, my faith blossomed and flourished, strengthened by the divine revelations I received through the words of the prophets in the Bible. With each passing day, I delved deeper into the sacred texts, hungry for the wisdom and guidance they contained.

It was during one of these fervent prayer sessions that I felt a stirring in my spirit, a gentle nudge from the Holy Spirit guiding me toward a new revelation. I was led to explore the teachings of Prophet TB Joshua, a name unfamiliar to me until that moment.

Intrigued by this divine prompting, I turned to YouTube in search of more information about Prophet TB Joshua and his ministry. As I listened to his sermons and testimonies, I was captivated by the depth of his insights and the power of his words.

Here was a man, much like the prophets of the Old Testament, who spoke with authority and conviction, channeling divine wisdom and revelation to guide and uplift those in need. His message resonated deeply with me, offering a fresh perspective on faith and spirituality that ignited a fire within my soul.

In Prophet TB Joshua, I found a beacon of light and truth, a modern-day vessel through which God's word was made manifest in the world. His teachings inspired me to deepen my connection with God and to embrace my role as a spiritual warrior in the ongoing battle against the forces of darkness.

As I continued to immerse myself in his teachings and ministry, my faith soared to new heights, fueled by the knowledge that God's prophets were indeed alive and well in the world today. Though he deceased in the few years that past. For, if God had prophets in the past, why not now? Truly, God is the same yesterday, today, and forever, and His word endures throughout the ages.

With Prophet TB Joshua's teaching as my new guide, I embarked on a journey of spiritual growth and enlightenment, confident in the knowledge that God's divine plan was unfolding in my life in ways I could never have imagined. As I walked this path of faith and obedience, I knew that I was destined for greatness, empowered by the presence of God's prophets in my life.

As I delved deeper into the teachings of Prophet TB Joshua through his YouTube videos, I was awestruck by the miraculous wonders of God that unfolded before my eyes. But it wasn't just the miracles that captivated me; it was the profound wisdom and insight contained within his teachings that resonated deeply with my soul.

I found myself drawn to his messages of forgiveness and sacrifice, principles that he exemplified in his own life with unwavering dedication. Prophet TB Joshua lived a life of sacrifice, consistently giving his time, resources, and wealth to help those in need. His selflessness and generosity were evident to all who knew him, and his impact on the world was immeasurable.

As I studied his teachings, I was inspired to emulate his example of sacrificial living, to give of myself freely and generously to others, just as he had done. As I watched his spiritual sons carry on his legacy, I marveled at the power and authority they wielded in their own right, each one a reflection of their mentor's teachings and values.

But even as I immersed myself in the teachings of Prophet TB Joshua and his spiritual sons, my health continued to deteriorate, casting a shadow of uncertainty over my life. Despite my unwavering faith and devotion, the relentless march of illness threatened to dim the light of hope that burned within me.

Yet, even in the midst of my physical suffering, I found solace and strength in the teachings of Prophet TB Joshua, knowing that God's power was made perfect in my weakness. And though my body may have been frail, my spirit remained steadfast, anchored in the unwavering faith that God's plans for me were greater than any trial or tribulation I faced.

Prophet Lovy Elias

It was a surprising turn of events when I stumbled upon Prophet Lovy's video on my Facebook feed. Though I typically avoided listening to unfamiliar spiritual leaders, something about him drew me in. With a sense of curiosity and intrigue, I clicked on his video, unsure of what to expect.

In the first few minutes of listening to him speak, I was captivated. His words seemed to flow like liquid gold, carrying a depth and resonance that struck a chord within me. I found myself hanging onto his every word, hungry for more of the profound wisdom he imparted.

Recognizing the value of his teachings, I decided to delve deeper into his content. Preferring not to spend excessive time on Facebook, I sought out his YouTube channel and subscribed. Over the course of the next two months, I dedicated two hours every night to listening to Prophet Lovy's teachings.

What I discovered in his messages was unlike anything I had encountered before. The revelations he shared were profound, offering new insights and perspectives that resonated deeply with me. It was as if a veil had been lifted, revealing truths I had never before considered.

Through Prophet Lovy's teachings, I found myself embarking on a transformative journey of spiritual growth and enlightenment. His words became a source of inspiration and guidance, leading me closer to a deeper understanding of myself and my faith.

As I continued to absorb his teachings, I felt a profound sense of gratitude for the unexpected blessing of encountering Prophet Lovy. His presence in my generation had opened up new avenues of spiritual exploration, enriching my journey in ways I never could have imagined.

In the meantime, I had to go for an outpatient cardiac biopsy. As the medical specialists continued their efforts to uncover the root cause of my severe health condition, they determined that biopsies were necessary. Despite initial reassurances of a same-day discharge, I found myself unexpectedly admitted to the hospital for the procedure.

However, what was meant to be a routine biopsy took a drastic turn. Something went terribly wrong, and I was swiftly transferred to the ICU, where I spent the next three days in a precarious state. In that harrowing moment, I came face to face with death itself.

Despite the gravity of the situation, I was strangely filled with a sense of calm assurance that everything would ultimately be alright. But while I maintained my composure, I couldn't ignore the fear and anxiety etched on the face of my only son. His concern for my well-being weighed heavily on my heart, amplifying the gravity of the situation.

My cousin

Meanwhile, my cousin Phelet Cameau, who resided in Montreal, Canada, was overwhelmed with stress as he grappled with the situation from afar. The physical distance only compounded the emotional strain, leaving him feeling helpless and distraught in the face of my health crisis.

During this tumultuous period, my cousin Phelet stepped into a role that transcended mere familial ties—he became a beacon of hope and strength, a guiding light in the midst of darkness. Though he may not have been a known prophet in the traditional sense, his unwavering faith and steadfast support played a prophetic role in my life during this trying time.

With each passing day, Phelet's words of encouragement became a lifeline, a reminder to hold fast to my faith and trust in God's unfailing grace. "Cousine, everything will be alright," he would reassure me, his words infused with a quiet confidence that echoed the promises of divine providence.

But Phelet's role as a spiritual support went beyond mere words—he was a constant presence by my side, offering prayers, songs of praise, and moments of levity to lift my spirits. His unwavering commitment to my well-being was evident in every gesture and word of encouragement, as he tirelessly stood by me in my darkest hour.

In the midnight hours, when despair threatened to overwhelm me, Phelet provided sustenance for my soul, offering psalms and songs to soothe my troubled mind. His references became like nourishing snacks for my spirit, providing comfort and strength to sustain me through the long, lonely nights.

Through his unwavering support and encouragement, Phelet embodied the essence of a true man of God—a vessel through which God's love and compassion flowed freely. In his presence, I found solace and reassurance, knowing that I was not alone in my struggles and that God's presence was ever near.

Though he may not have held the title of a prophet, Phelet's role in my life during this difficult time was nothing short of prophetic. He guided me with wisdom, comforted me with love, and strengthened me with his unwavering faith. And for that, I will be forever grateful.

Chapter VII: Getting the final diagnosis

Following my discharge from the hospital ICU unit, I eagerly awaited my scheduled appointment with a cardiologist and an oncologist, where I would finally receive the crucial results of the biopsies conducted on my heart and bone marrow. The anticipation weighed heavily on my mind as I navigated the days leading up to the appointment, grappling with a mixture of anxiety and hope.

Back at home, amidst the uncertainty surrounding my health, I found solace in the familiar routine of engaging in personal bible study sessions and in warfare prayer with Prophet Lovy online. Day after day, I immersed myself in spiritual warfare, drawing strength from the powerful messages and teachings that resonated deeply within me. With each prayer session, I felt my spiritual strength grow, forging a deeper connection with God and His divine purpose for my life.

Despite the persistent deterioration of my physical health, I refused to allow despair to overshadow my faith. Instead, I leaned into my relationship with God, seeking refuge in His presence and finding comfort in His promises. In the midst of my struggles, I discovered a profound sense of peace and assurance, knowing that I was not alone in my journey.

As the day of my oncologist appointment drew nearer, I clung to the hope that awaited me, trusting in God's plan for my life, whatever the outcome may be. And though the road ahead was uncertain, I found strength in the knowledge that my faith would sustain me through every trial and tribulation.

As I sat in the lobby, awaiting my appointment with the oncologist, my mind raced with a whirlwind of emotions. I couldn't help but observe the other patients around me, each bearing the weight of their own health struggles. Despite their weariness, I couldn't ignore the stark contrast between them and myself. While they appeared worn and weathered, I stood out as the youngest among them, a stark reminder of the fragility of youth amidst the challenges of illness.

In that moment, instead of succumbing to feelings of despair or self-pity, I made a conscious choice to shift my perspective. Rather than dwelling on the unfortunate circumstances that brought us all together in that waiting room, I chose to focus on the resilience and determination that burned within me.

I refused to see myself as a victim of circumstance. Instead, I embraced the belief that I would emerge from this trial stronger and more resilient than ever before. With unwavering faith and determination, I resolved to face whatever news the oncologist had for me with courage and grace.

In that moment of clarity, I realized that my journey was not defined by the challenges I faced, but by the strength and resilience I possessed in overcoming them. As I prepared to meet with the oncologist, I carried with me a sense of hope and optimism, knowing that no matter the outcome, I would face it head-on with unwavering resolve.

As my name was called, signaling it was time to meet with the doctor, a wave of anxiety washed over me. Steeling myself for the news to come, I entered the room with a mixture of trepidation and resolve. Little did I know the words that awaited me would shatter my world.

As the doctor delivered the diagnosis of cardiac amyloidosis and multiple myeloma, the weight of the news hit me like a ton of bricks. In that moment, devastation threatened to consume me, but amidst the darkness, a glimmer of hope flickered.

Summoning every ounce of courage within me, I lifted my head and met the doctor's gaze, my voice steady as I posed the question that hung heavily in the air: "What now?"

Though the road ahead appeared daunting and uncertain, I refused to allow despair to dictate my response. Instead, I chose to confront the challenges before me with a spirit of determination and resilience. In that moment of vulnerability, I found strength in the simple act of facing adversity head-on, ready to navigate the journey ahead with courage and grace.

As the doctor outlined the proposed treatment plan, detailing a rigorous schedule of chemotherapy sessions spanning six months, I listened intently, absorbing every word with a calm demeanor. Despite the gravity of the situation, I remained remarkably composed, much to the doctor's apparent surprise.

Sensing my seemingly subdued reaction, the doctor attempted to impress upon me the severity of my condition, emphasizing the gravity of being diagnosed with multiple myeloma, a formidable adversary in the form of cancer. His words carried a weighty urgency, as if he sought to cast a spell of fear and apprehension over me.

Yet, in the midst of his impassioned plea, I maintained a stoic silence, my inner resolve unshaken. Deep within the recesses of my heart, I found solace in a quiet mantra: "This too shall pass." With each repetition, I anchored myself in the unwavering belief that no matter the challenges I faced, they were but temporary trials on the path to eventual healing and renewal.

Accepting that trust in the Lord does not guarantee the end that you want.

Indeed, accepting that trust in the Lord does not guarantee the fulfillment of our desires, but rather the alignment with His will, is a profound aspect of faith. Here are some insights on embracing this aspect of trust

Trusting in the Lord means surrendering our own desires and plans to His greater wisdom and understanding. It involves acknowledging that God's plans may differ from our own, but His ways are ultimately for our highest good.

Learn to find peace in surrender to God. When we let go of our need to control outcomes and instead surrender to God's will, we can find a deeper sense of peace and acceptance, even in the midst of uncertainty or difficulty.

Trusting in the Lord means trusting in His perfect timing. Sometimes, what we want may not happen when or how we expect it to, but we can trust that God's timing is always perfect and that He knows what is best for us.

Embracing God's will over our own desires requires a deepening of faith and trust. It's a journey of growth and spiritual maturity, where we learn to lean on God's understanding rather than our own limited perspective.

Continuously seek His guidance through prayer, meditation so that we can align our hearts and minds with God's will. By listening to His voice and following His leading, we can walk confidently in the path He has set before us.

Know that trusting in the Lord's will means finding purpose and meaning in every circumstance, even those that may seem challenging or difficult. It's about recognizing that God can use every situation for our growth and His glory.

Keep an open heart to His Blessings. Understand that when we surrender to God's will, we open ourselves up to His blessings, which may come in unexpected ways. By letting go of our own expectations, we allow God to work in our lives in ways that exceed our imagination.

Reflecting on God's faithfulness in the past can strengthen our trust in His will for the future. Remembering God's goodness, even when things don't go according to our plans. Can trust that God is with us, guiding us every step of the way.

Ultimately, trusting in the Lord's will requires a deepening of our relationship with Him, a willingness to surrender our own desires, and a steadfast faith that His plans for us are good and purposeful. For God's grace never fails.

Chapter VIII

Though the doctor's words echoed in my mind, I refused to allow fear to take root within me. Instead, I embraced a sense of inner peace and steadfast determination, knowing that with each step of the journey, I would emerge stronger and more resilient than before. In that moment of silent moment, I found the strength to face whatever lay ahead with unwavering faith and courage.

With a brave and humble strength, I mustered the courage to express my decision to the doctor: I would not begin treatment immediately, opting instead to commence chemotherapy a month later. Though reluctant, the doctor agreed to my request, albeit with a palpable sense of reservation.

In the interim, I wasted no time in taking action. Securing my airplane ticket, I embarked on a journey to Simi Valley, California, where Revelation Church, led by Papa Lo, awaited. With each step towards this new chapter, I felt a surge of strength and empowerment coursing through me, as if guided by an unseen hand.

In the embrace of this newfound determination, I knew instinctively that I was on the right path. Despite the uncertainties that lay ahead, I found solace in the belief that I was being guided by forces greater than myself, navigating me toward a destination imbued with hope and healing.

As I embarked on this transformative journey, I carried with me a sense of faith and resilience, ready to embrace the challenges and opportunities that awaited. In the sanctuary of Revelation Church, I sought not only solace but also renewal, knowing that within its hallowed halls lay the potential for spiritual and physical restoration.

Visiting revelation church

As I arrived at Revelation Church, I found myself amidst a sea of eager worshippers, patiently waiting in line for hours prior to the doors opening. The anticipation hung thick in the air, palpable with the collective energy of hope and faith that permeated the atmosphere.

Despite the discomfort of standing in line for an extended period, I couldn't help but notice a remarkable change within myself. The swelling in my ankle, a constant reminder of my health struggles, remained stagnant, defying the usual pattern of deterioration. It was as if divine intervention had momentarily stilled the progression of my ailment, offering a glimmer of respite amidst the tumult of uncertainty.

Moreover, I found myself enveloped in a profound sense of joy and contentment, as if I had stepped into my true element. Surrounded by fellow believers, each radiating with hope and expectation, I felt a renewed sense of purpose and belonging. Together, we shared in the collective experience of prayer and praise, invoking the might of God to manifest in our midst.

In those sacred moments of communion, I was reminded of the transformative power of faith and community. Amidst the trials and tribulations of life, we found strength in our unity, drawing upon the boundless grace and mercy of a loving Creator. And as we lifted our voices in prayer and worship, I knew with unwavering certainty that miracles were unfolding, both within and around us, ushering in a tide of hope and healing.

As I immersed myself in the atmosphere of Revelation Church, I was consumed by a deep longing to encounter the divine. Little did I know, God had orchestrated a divine appointment for me within those hallowed halls. In a moment that left me awe-struck, Prophet Lovy singled me out and began to speak with a profound clarity that resonated to the depths of my soul.

With unwavering conviction, Prophet Lovy recounted the car accident I had endured with my parents over a decade ago. As he delved into the depths of my past, he unearthed a truth that had long lain buried beneath layers of grief and trauma. It was a revelation that left me speechless, for in that moment, I realized that God had located me within the very walls of the church.

Through Prophet Lovy's discernment, I came to understand that the aftermath of the car accident had left me vulnerable to spiritual attacks, allowing darkness to take root within my soul. It was a revelation that struck at the core of my being, unveiling the hidden wounds that had festered within me for years.

For so long, I had carried the weight of my grief and trauma, unable to release the pain and sorrow that consumed me. Dreams of my parents, especially my mother, haunted me relentlessly, serving as a constant reminder of the loss I had endured.

But in that sacred moment of revelation, I realized that God was offering me a path to healing and deliverance. Through the prayers and intercession of Prophet Lovy and the congregation, I found the courage to confront the darkness that had plagued me for so long, trusting in God's promise to bring restoration and wholeness to my wounded soul.

As Papa Lo prayed for me, invoking the prophetic power bestowed upon him by God, I felt an immediate sense of relief wash over me like a gentle wave. It was as if a heavy burden had been lifted from my shoulders, and I could feel the presence of God enveloping me in His loving embrace. Overcome with emotion, tears streamed down my cheeks as I poured out my heart to the Lord in gratitude and surrender.

Leaving the church that night, my spirit was ablaze with a newfound faith and conviction. Though Prophet Lovy had not explicitly mentioned my illness, I knew deep within my soul that I had been touched by the hand of God, and that healing was already underway. With each step I took, I felt myself moving closer to the other side of my ordeal, basking in the assurance that victory was within reach.

As I journeyed forward with a heart full of faith, I found myself compelled to praise and magnify the name of the Lord, knowing that He alone held the power to transform my circumstances and lead me into a season of restoration and renewal. Though the road ahead may be fraught with challenges, I faced it with unwavering confidence, secure in the knowledge that with God by my side, I would emerge triumphant.

Attention

Don't allow anyone to deter you from following God's guidance. While some may question why you need to go to a specific place like California when God is everywhere, it's important to remember that each person's path is unique and ordained by God.

Throughout the Bible, we see examples of people seeking out specific locations or individuals in pursuit of God's blessings and healing. From lining up along roads where disciples passed (Acts 3) to waiting by the pool of Bethesda (John 5) to traveling from distant lands to find Jesus (Luke 7), the Scriptures illustrate the importance of following the leading of the Holy Spirit, even if it means going to unfamiliar places to receive deliverance.

In God's kingdom, there is a divine order and purpose for each believer. While all believers have access to the Holy Spirit and the general power from the Father, some are called to specific missions and are endowed with the necessary power from God to fulfill them. In many cases, God may lead us to His chosen servants to receive specific grace.

So, despite what others may believe, recognize that we are not all the same in the Kingdom. Each of us has a unique role to play in God's plan, and it's essential to remain obedient to His leading, trusting that He will equip us with everything we need to fulfil our divine purpose.

Ways to avoid the snares of the enemy

Seeking to avoid the snares of the enemy requires vigilance, wisdom, and spiritual discernment. In various religious teachings and philosophical traditions, the concept of spiritual warfare is often discussed, emphasizing the importance of recognizing and resisting negative influences and temptations.

Cultivate a strong spiritual foundation with your savior, Jesus, through prayer, meditation, and studying sacred texts. This can help strengthen your connection with your beliefs and provide guidance in discerning right from wrong.

Guard your mind and heart by refusing to let the enemy penetrate the thoughts and emotions you entertain. Negative thoughts and feelings can pave the way for the enemy's influence. Practice mindfulness and focus on uplifting and positive thoughts.

Continue to surround yourself with like-minded individuals who share your values and beliefs. Having a supportive community can provide encouragement, accountability, and protection against negative influences.

Develop the ability to discern between what is of light and what is of darkness. Trust your intuition and seek guidance from spiritual mentors or leaders when faced with difficult decisions. Romans 12: 1, "Do not conform yourself to this age, so that you may discern what is the will of God".

Regularly reflect on your actions, motivations, and behaviors. Acknowledge areas where you may be vulnerable to the enemy's snares and take proactive steps to strengthen your defenses. Psalms 119: 11 "I have stored up your word in my heart, that I might not sin against you".

Armor Yourself Spiritually, the concept of spiritual armor, symbolizing protection against spiritual attacks. Ephesians 6:12 says, "For we wrestle not against principalities, against powers, against the rulers of the darkness of this world, against spiritual wickedness in high places." These spiritual practices involve visualizing yourself surrounded by light, saying protective prayers, or reciting psalms.

Remain Humble and Grounded. For pride and arrogance can make one susceptible to the enemy's influence. Cultivate humility in your beliefs, acknowledging your limitations and seeking guidance from a higher power.

Again, I want to emphasize forgiveness and love; they are powerful tools against darkness. Cultivate a spirit of forgiveness towards yourself and others, and strive to embody love and compassion in all your interactions.

Be gentle and compassionate with yourself when anxiety arises. Remind yourself that it's normal to experience fear and worry, but also recognize your ability to overcome these feelings with God's help.

By incorporating these practices into your life, you can strengthen your spiritual defenses and navigate the challenges of life with greater resilience and discernment.

Chapter IX: Go along with the treatment

As I made my way back to the doctor's office to commence the treatment plan outlined by the oncologist, there was a palpable shift in my mindset. This time, I approached the situation with a steadfast faith that transcended any lingering anxiety. Despite the gravity of the circumstances, my unwavering belief in God's guiding hand imbued me with a sense of calm assurance.

Upon entering the treatment clinic, I felt compelled to reach out to a woman of God, a complete stranger, who had previously prophesied over me during my time at the Revelation church. As we engaged in conversation, she offered to pray for me, a gesture I accepted wholeheartedly. To my astonishment, she began to utter my exact diagnosis in her prayer, prophesying with unwavering certainty that I would emerge victorious in this battle. My God is awesome.

In that moment, I was overcome by a profound sense of reassurance and divine presence. It was as though God Himself was affirming His sovereignty over my situation, assuring me that I was not alone in my struggle. With each word of prayer spoken over me, I felt a renewed strength and resolve coursing through my veins, empowering me to face whatever lay ahead with unwavering courage and faith.

On the first morning of my treatment, I reached out to the woman of God who had previously prophesied over me. As we prayed together, she directed me to Psalm 139, offering words of encouragement and reminding me that it was natural to feel apprehensive about the treatment. Yet, she assured me that regardless of my cautiousness, I would overcome.

In that moment of prayer, she spoke another prophecy, one that would later come to fruition in my life. It was a powerful reminder of the faithfulness of God and His presence in every aspect of my journey. Truly, my God is awesome.

As I settled into the clinic chair, the sterile surroundings contrasting sharply with the turmoil within me, I couldn't escape the sensation of the IV needle piercing my skin, a tangible reminder of the battle raging inside my body. With each drop of medication seeping into my veins, I felt the weight of its side effects bearing down on me, threatening to overwhelm my senses.

In that moment of discomfort, I made a conscious decision to confront the emotional turmoil simmering within me. Closing my eyes against the clinical glare, I embarked on a journey of introspection. With each breath, I whispered confessions, my words a humble offering to a higher power. I poured out my heart in prayer, seeking solace in the midst of uncertainty, my petitions a beacon of hope in the dimly lit room.

But it was forgiveness that truly set me free. With a trembling voice, I uttered the names of those who had wronged me, each syllable a testament to my resolve to release the burden of resentment. One by one, I let go of the hurt and the grief, allowing the healing balm of forgiveness to mend the wounds that lingered within my soul.

As I surrendered to the cathartic release of forgiveness, a profound sense of peace washed over me. In the quiet of that clinic room, amidst the hum of medical equipment and the rhythmic drip of the IV, I felt the stirring of reassurance within my spirit. It was as though a voice whispered softly in the depths of my being, reminding me that I was not alone, that I was already a conqueror in the face of adversity.

However, at the beginning of my treatment, my condition worsened. I could not sleep day or night and felt like I was drowning in my own body fluid. The shortness of breath became worse. I was confined to a chair daily. I could clearly notice the uncertainty in the face of my doctors. But suddenly, there was a shift.

The swift response of my body to the treatment was nothing short of miraculous. Within a mere month of initiating the regimen prescribed by the medical team, my blood markers plummeted to levels close to normal. It was a development that left the treatment team, astounded and incredulous. While they marveled at the unexpected efficacy of the treatment, I couldn't shake the overwhelming sense that a divine hand was at work behind the scenes.

As I reflected on the rapid improvement in my health, I couldn't help but marvel at the intricacies of divine intervention. It was as though God Himself had intervened in the course of my illness, guiding the medication to its intended target with unerring precision. In the face of such undeniable evidence of divine providence, I found myself humbled and awestruck by the magnitude of God's power and grace.

While I expressed gratitude to the medical team for their expertise and dedication, I knew in the depths of my soul that this victory was not solely of human making. It was a testament to the boundless mercy and compassion of a loving God who had chosen to intervene in my life, transforming what seemed like an insurmountable obstacle into a triumph of faith and healing.

Attention

No matter how challenging life gets, never lose sight of God. Life is full of ups and downs, and it's easy to get caught up in the turmoil. Yet, it's in these moments of adversity that our faith is tested and strengthened. Remember, even when human efforts seem to help or fail, everything ultimately happens through God's guidance and grace. His plans are higher than our plans, and His ways are beyond our understanding.

Keep your faith strong and trust in God's plan for you. It's essential to remember that we are not alone in our struggles. God is always with us, offering His strength and support. As it is written in Philippians 4:13, "I can do all things through Christ who gives me strength." This verse is a powerful reminder that our strength does not come from our own abilities, but from Christ who empowers us.

By His Spirit, we receive the strength we need to face any challenge. This divine strength enables us to persevere, even when situations seem insurmountable. The Apostle Paul, who endured immense hardships, encourages us with his words that it is through Christ's power that we can overcome.

Cultivate walking by faith, not by sight. This means trusting in God's promises and His unseen hand guiding our lives. Walking by faith requires us to rely not on our own understanding but on God's wisdom and timing. It's a call to trust God fully, even when we cannot see the outcome.

Furthermore, hold onto the promise found in Romans 8:28, "And we know that in all things God works for the good of those who love Him, who have been called according to His purpose." This verse reassures us that God is at work in every situation, orchestrating events for our ultimate good. Even when we face trials and tribulations, we can have confidence that God is using these experiences to shape us and fulfill His divine purpose in our lives.

In every situation, lean on your faith. Trust in God's wisdom and believe in His plan for your life. His guidance will provide you with the strength and perseverance you need to overcome any obstacle. Remember that God is our refuge and strength, an ever-present help in times of trouble. Through faith, we can find peace and assurance that no matter what happens, God is in control and working all things together for our good.

Chapter X: Surprising turn around

Several months later, there was a remarkable turnaround in my health as my blood markers returned to normal. I was able to work out again with ease. It's worth noting the initial prognosis from the doctor, who anticipated a regimen of weekly treatment for six months, followed by ongoing monthly treatment for life. However, God had a different plan in mind.

After just three and a half months, led by God, I made the decision to halt the treatment. While my doctor initially expressed reluctance, they eventually agreed to monitor my progress through monthly blood tests. As the months passed, I experienced steady improvement in my condition without the treatment.

Month after month, I witnessed tangible signs of recovery and restoration. It was a testament to the power of faith and perseverance. Through it all, I remained steadfast in my belief in God's healing presence and continued to confess His healing over me.

This journey taught me the importance of trusting in God's timing and guidance, even in the face of medical uncertainty. It reinforced my conviction that miracles can happen when we place our faith in the divine and take courageous steps forward.

By God's grace, no relapse was suspected, and for over a year, I continued to overcome without any treatment. It was a testament to His unwavering support and mercy. However, unexpectedly, I experienced a recurrence of the symptoms one night after going to sleep.

In the darkness of the midnight hour, I found myself once again battling the illness. But amidst the struggle, there came a profound moment. Following a midnight prayer session, I had a vivid dream. In this dream, I witnessed people preparing for surgery, with one of my deceased brother seemingly poised to operate on them.

Yet, in the dream, I firmly declared, "No one will operate on me." In a moment of divine inspiration, I took hold of a large syringe with a formidable needle. With unwavering resolve, I inserted it into my heart and drew out copious amounts of fluid.

Since that surreal moment, all the symptoms miraculously vanished. It was the divine intervention that had taken place, restoring me to health once more. This experience reaffirmed my belief in the power of prayer, faith, and divine guidance. It was a reminder that even in the darkest of times, God's grace is ever-present, offering healing and redemption beyond human comprehension.

Reflection

Beloved, when the Almighty bestows upon you the victory, it is imperative to grasp it firmly, not merely in the physical realm, but also in the spiritual domain. Understand that divine blessings are not capricious; they are bestowed with purpose and conviction. When God declares healing, it is not a fleeting promise but an immutable truth.

Indeed, the sacred scriptures Isaiah 53:5 affirm that through the stripes of Christ, healing is procured for His faithful disciples. Therefore, it is incumbent upon believers to wield the authority bestowed upon them by the indwelling Spirit of Christ. As heirs to the kingdom, we are vested with the power to decree and command in alignment with divine will.

Walking in the authority conferred by Jesus Christ requires a steadfast commitment to spiritual discipline and discernment. It entails an unwavering trust in the sovereignty of God and a resolute adherence to His Word. By embracing our identity as vessels of divine power, we can confront adversity with unwavering faith and confidence.

It is imperative to recognize that spiritual warfare is not waged with carnal weapons but with the potent arsenal of prayer, proclamation, and spiritual discernment. By tapping into the reservoir of divine power, believers can effectuate transformative change in their lives and circumstances.

Beloved, let us heed the exhortation to take hold of the promises of God with unwavering faith and authority. For in Christ, we are more than conquerors, endowed with the divine mandate to proclaim victory over every trial and tribulation. As we walk in the authority granted to us by our Savior, let us boldly declare the manifestation of God's blessings and provision in every aspect of our lives. As you stand firm in His truth, you can overcome any challenge and walk in the freedom and victory that He has provided.

Do not let our circumstances drown us. While it is okay to feel pain or to grieve, we cannot do so as the world does. The world has no hope, but we in Jesus Christ have eternal life. The enemy will take advantage of our agitation and frustration to lead us into more turmoil, while God never intended it to be that way. Most of the time, it is supposed to be a quick test for promotion in God's plan.

Our parents or loved ones may be dear to us, but they are not our Father, Lord, and Savior. Therefore, when the time comes for them to return to their Maker, it should not bring despair to the surviving loved ones. It is okay to grieve and to experience pain—life comes with challenges. However, remember that death is not the end. Diseases, despair, turmoil, and trials are not the end. God has the final say. He is always in control. For those who are in Christ – we will meet again.

God's guidance and the support of faithful brethren

As I reflect on my journey, knowing God's word, I recognize that this disease was nothing but a promotion test by God. Did I understand that at the time? No! I was suffering terribly, struck by numerous unfortunate situations and a sickness that showed no mercy. However, I thank the Holy Spirit, who held my hand through the storm. He did not let me go astray. On the contrary, this trial brought me closer to Jesus.

I continually thank God for my cousin Phelet, a true man of faith who stood by me and filled the gap when my own faith was weak. I remember his constant encouragement: "Keep the faith up, sing the hymn, read the psalms even when you do not feel like it. Trust me, God will see you through." Those were his words. His unwavering support was a lifeline during my darkest moments.

I am also deeply grateful for other spiritual brethren who interceded for me before the throne of grace when I needed it the most. Their prayers and support provided a solid foundation that helped me to endure and grow in faith. This collective spiritual support and the Holy Spirit's guidance transformed my suffering into a profound journey of spiritual growth and closer communion with God.

Reflecting on this period, I see clearly how God's grace and the steadfast faith of those around help me turn my trial into a testament of His enduring love and faithfulness. Through this experience, I learned the power of community, prayer, and the unwavering strength that comes from trusting in God's plan, even when it is not immediately clear.

A Testimony of Faith and Gratitude

Finally, I glorify God, my Lord, my Savior, my Redeemer. My Jehovah Rapha, Jireh, I worship You. My lips, my heart, my spirit, my entire being will never cease to adore You. As I promised in prayers through my suffering, I will make sure that as many people as I can hear this testimony when You pull me out of this ordeal. Notice that I did not say if He will, but when He will.

Psalm 116:12-14 says, "What shall I render to the Lord for all His benefits towards me? I will take the cup of salvation, and call upon the name of the Lord. I will pay my vows unto the Lord now in the presence of all His people."

Know that God is a merciful God. Trust in His goodness. According to His timing and His will, He will manifest His grace unto you.

Conclusion

The loss of my parents had a profound and destructive impact on me for a long time. To tell the truth, it was something I had always feared because my parents, especially my mother, meant everything to me. I dreamed of the day I could care for them and express my love, and seeing that dream cut short was devastating.

My parents were the only people I trusted completely. I believed no one on earth could love me as they did. Even though I have many siblings, that did not lessen my bond with my parents—in fact, it only strengthened it.

Imagine this: living with the grief of losing well-loved parents and many siblings, enduring a failed marriage, and becoming a single mother and provider. The load was intense and unbearable. On top of that, managing work, university workload, and the burdens of raising a child alone were overwhelming. The enemy exploited these afflictions to bring even more disaster. This is why the scriptures say, "Cast your burdens unto Him, for He cares for you." If you don't, the enemy will use those situations to take you down.

Don't make the mistake of being consumed by your circumstances, as I did for a while. Instead, surrender to God's promises and plan for you. Let God hold your hands and help you navigate through the storms. Beloved, no matter how devoted you are as a servant of Christ, you will face trials and despair. You will encounter situations that seem insurmountable and unrepairable. However, the purpose of this message is to assure you that God always has His ways and the final say.

I was told by the medical team that I would need treatment for six months and then monthly for the rest of my life. However, after just four months of treatment, I was healed by the miraculous hands of God. Since then, I have not been on any medication —glory to God. Please, do not ignore medical advice or your present situation, but rather seek the face of the Lord and His plans for you specifically. Remember, what God does for one, He can do for all. The scripture says, "I sent My word to heal your diseases." God's words cannot return to Him empty without fulfilling what they were sent to accomplish. Believe in His words and promises.

If you hold on to His words and promises, I am here to testify that God is faithful. He will fulfill His promises unto you. Keep your eyes on Him, and the waves of the sea will not drown you. Just like the rainbow appears after the rain, you will thrive. You will be directed by the Lord, and He will light up your life.

Beloved, it is all part of the journey—the good, the bad, and the ugly. Also, know that our Lord is in control. He will not mishandle our journey. The circumstances, trials, storms, diseases, and despair are all part of the teaching process. Do not delay the process; let it flow. Though it may be hard at times, trust the process and the Master Jesus. He will make it worth it according to His will and wishes. You will flourish, and you will testify of God's goodness.

Your journey will lead to a testimony.

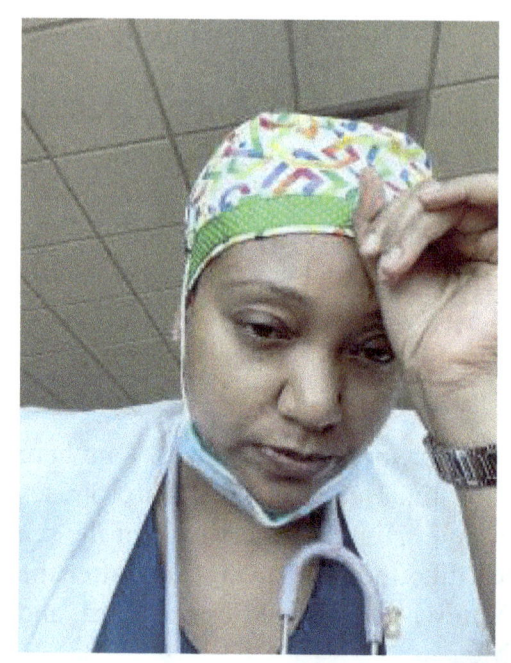

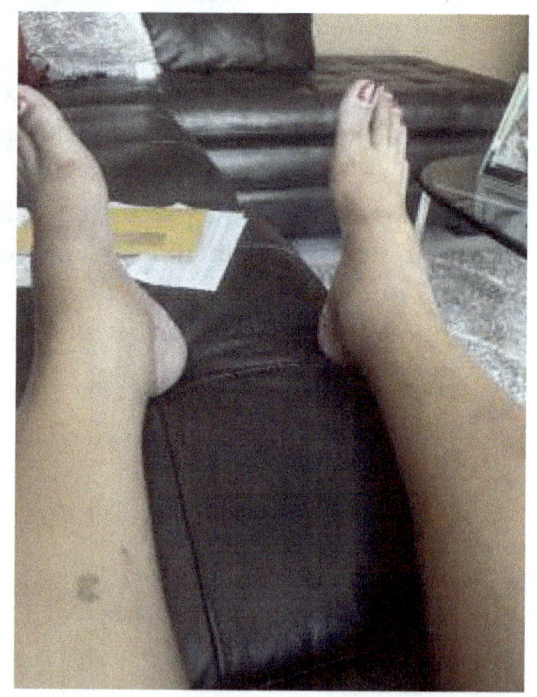

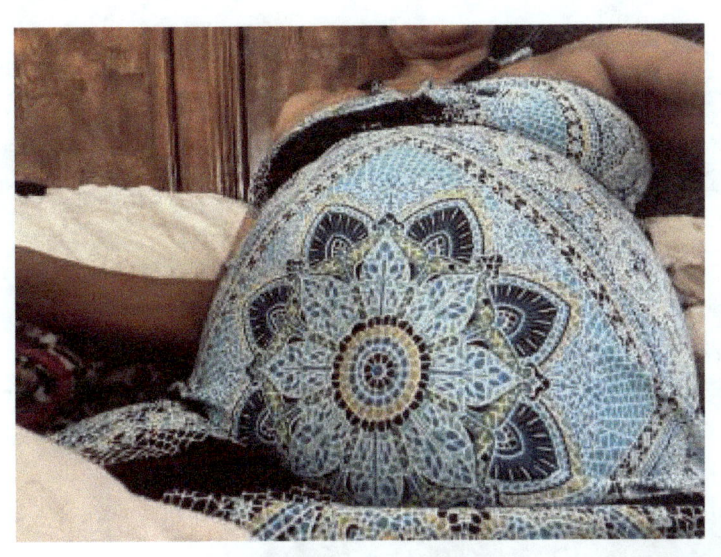

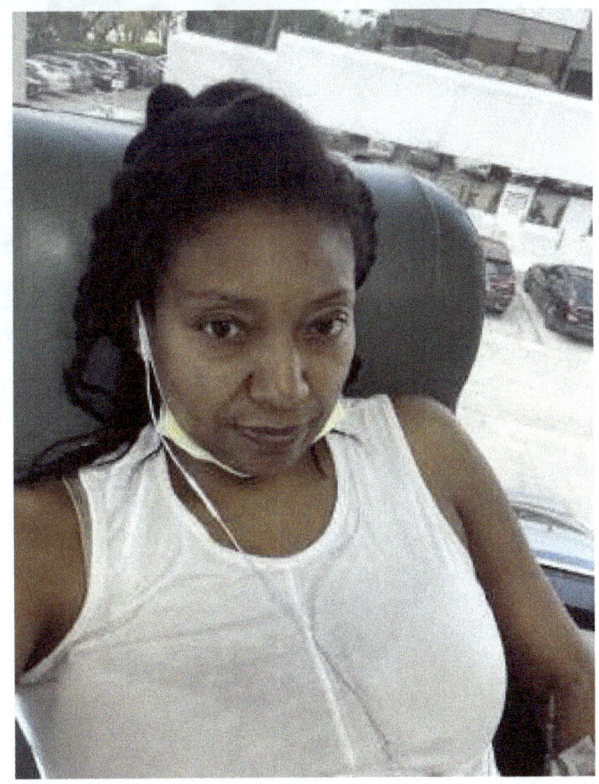

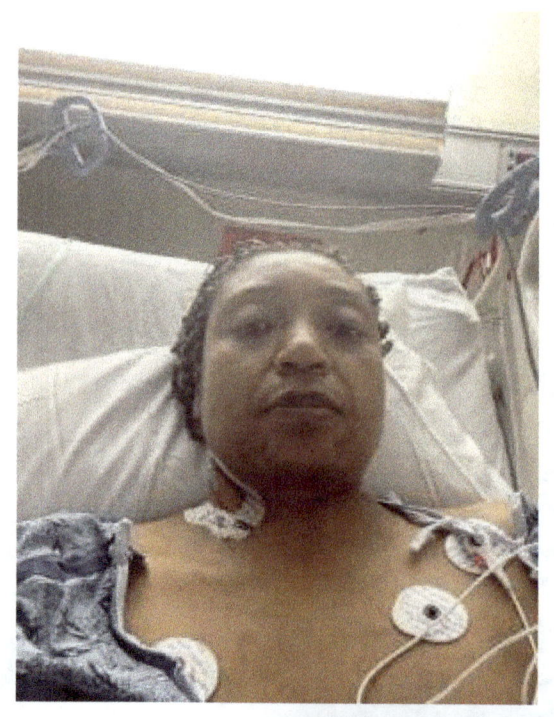

Prayer for the Sick

Father God, we thank You and glorify Your name. We bow before Your throne to revere You as we ask for forgiveness for our sins and shortcomings. By the power of Your blood, we are cleansed and washed, for there is no stain that the blood of Jesus cannot remove. By faith, we declare that we are holy, sanctified, saved, and whole as You have called us to be.

Our Father, we know that You hear us as You always have. Let this prayer activate new grace in the reader's life to face life, knowing that God has already orchestrated everything for our good. Help them to see through Your Spirit instead of analyzing things with their carnal minds. Increase their faith to please You, for no one can please You without faith.

Whatever tragedy they face, whether it is unknown illnesses, lingering symptoms, incurable diseases, family loss, divorce, or any other hardship, let them experience Your invisible hands in their situations. Father, throughout my life, (Isaiah 59:1) *Behold the Lord's hands is not too short to save, nor His ear too dull, that He can not hear.* Your invisible hand has never left me, though sometimes I felt lost until You led whatever situation I was into a testimony. Let this prayer be a starting point for anyone who reads it and is in need of a divine intervention.

I pray that You show this reader mercy. As we thank You and praise You, we believe that it is already done in Jesus's name.

Amen.